THE EARLY LITERACY COMPANY

Author Gail Nordstrand, Reading Specialist.

Illustrations Belinda Carter, Artist.

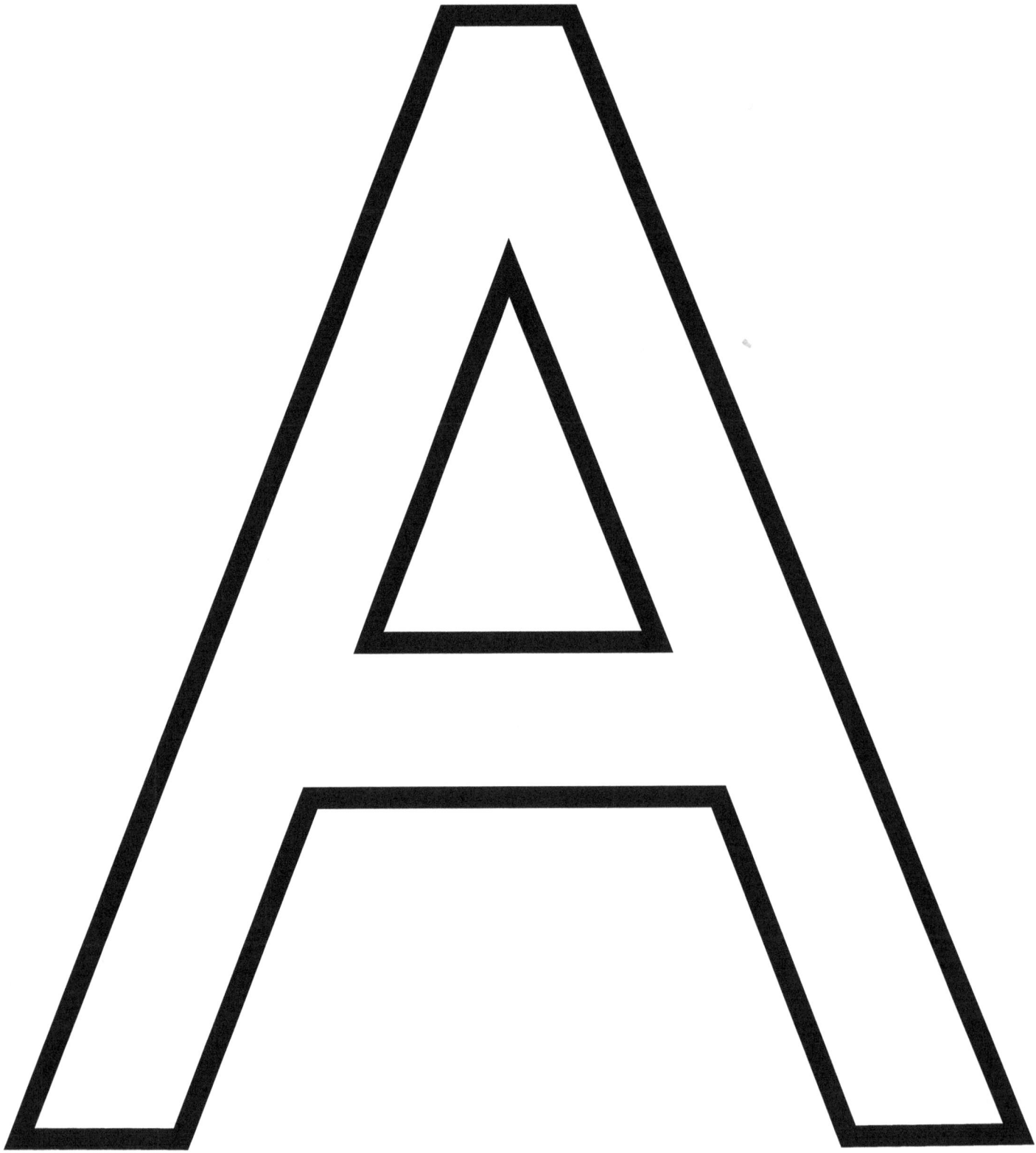

A

Alligator

B

Bunny

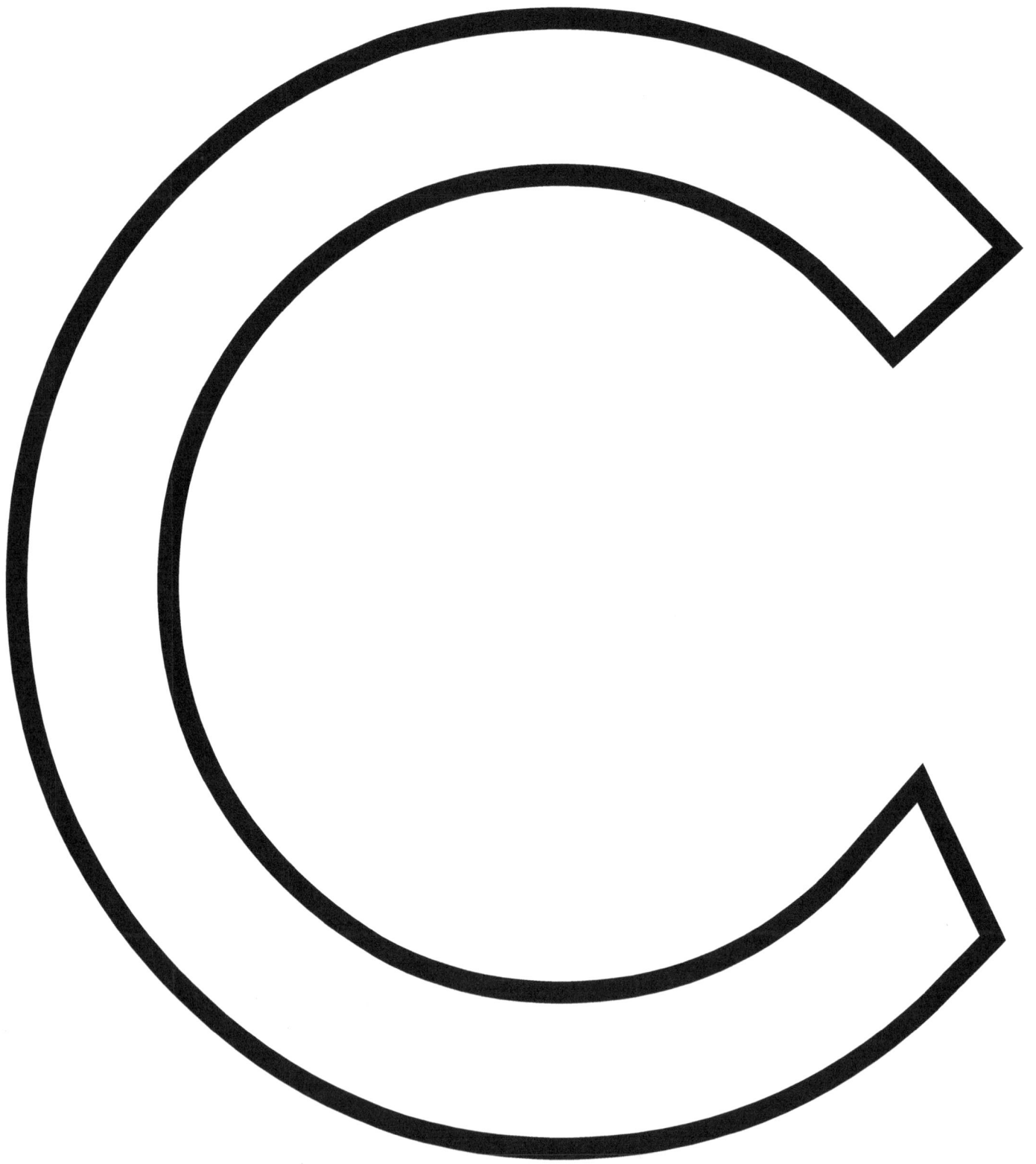

C

Cow

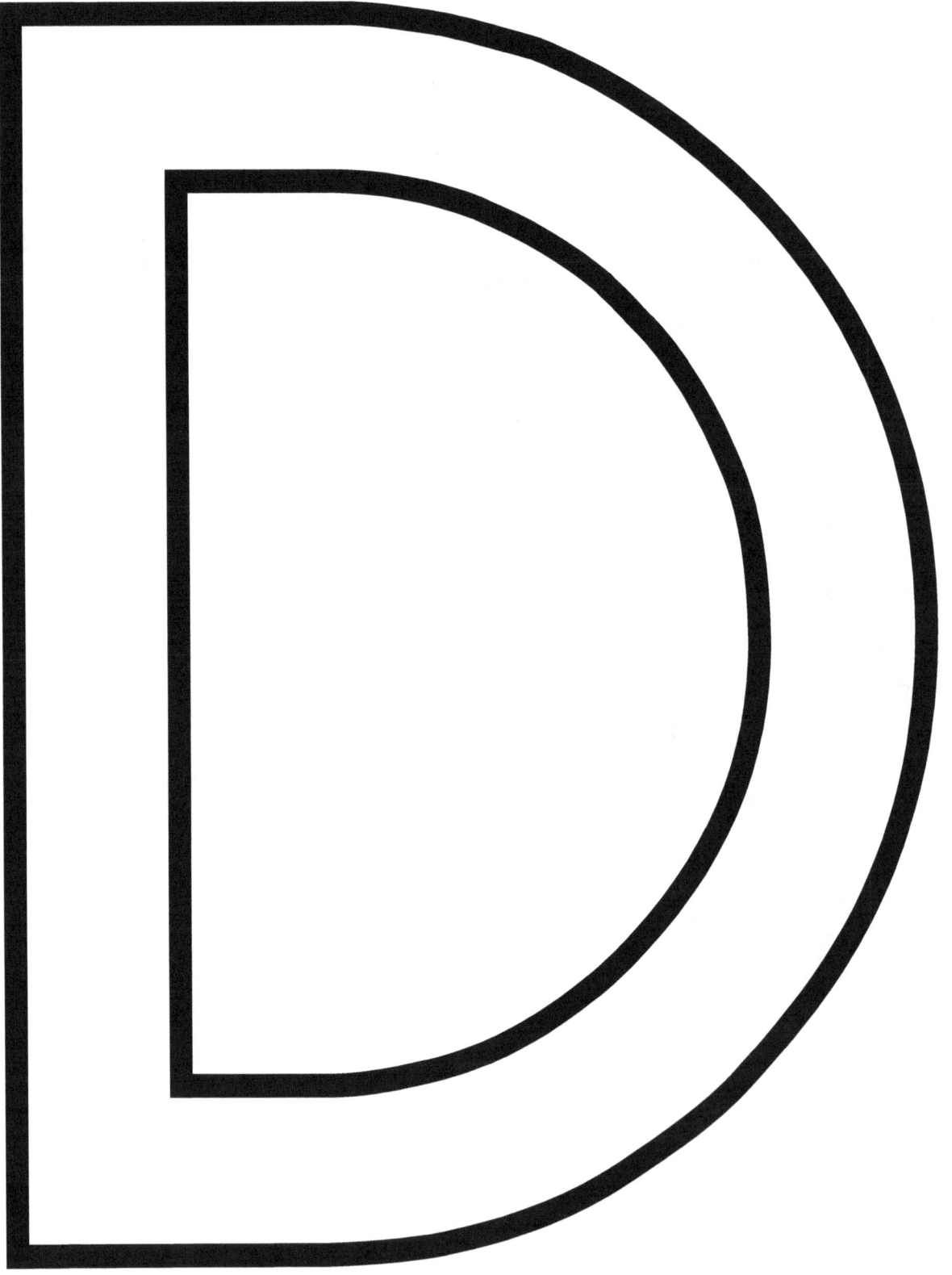

Dolphin

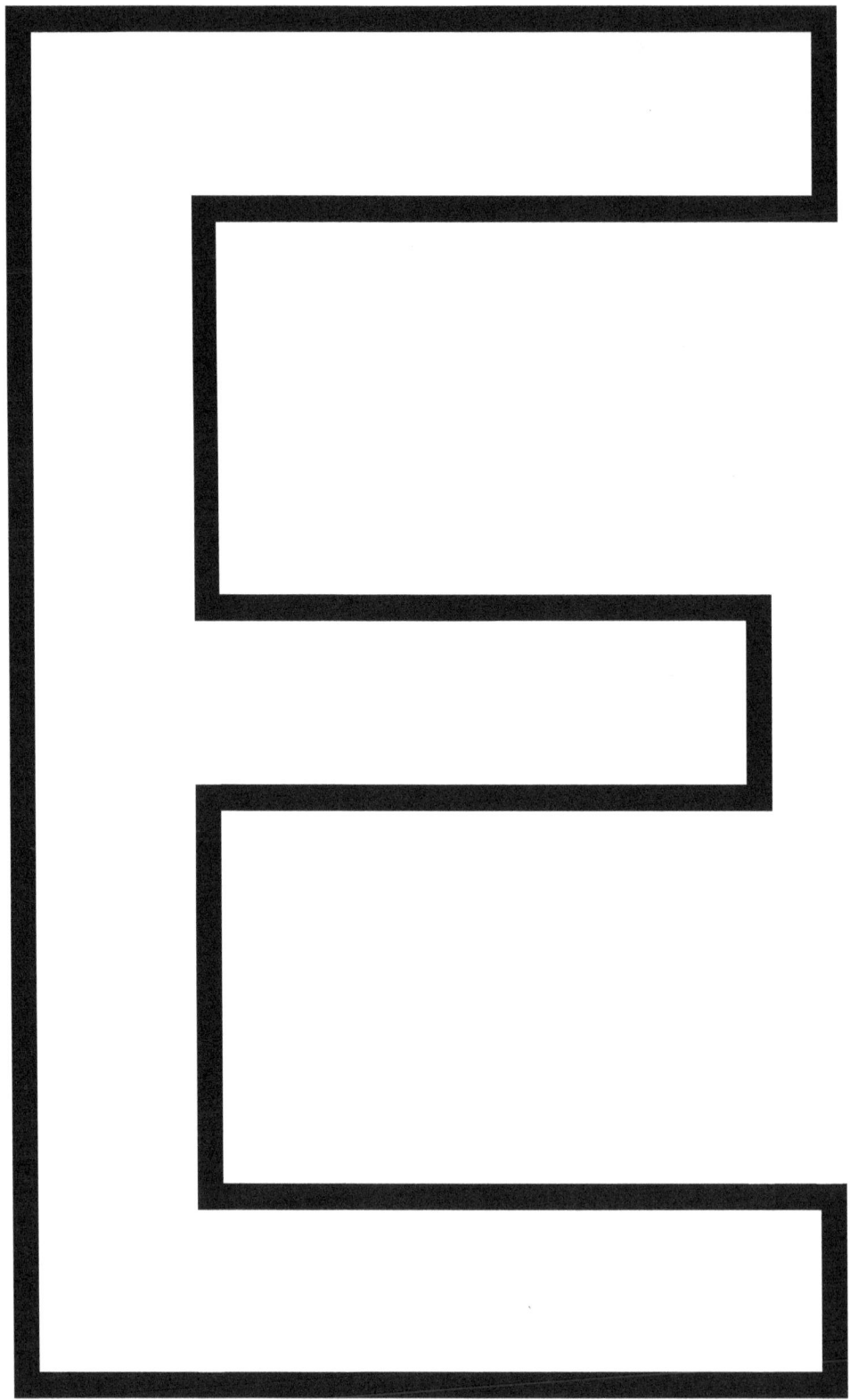

Emu

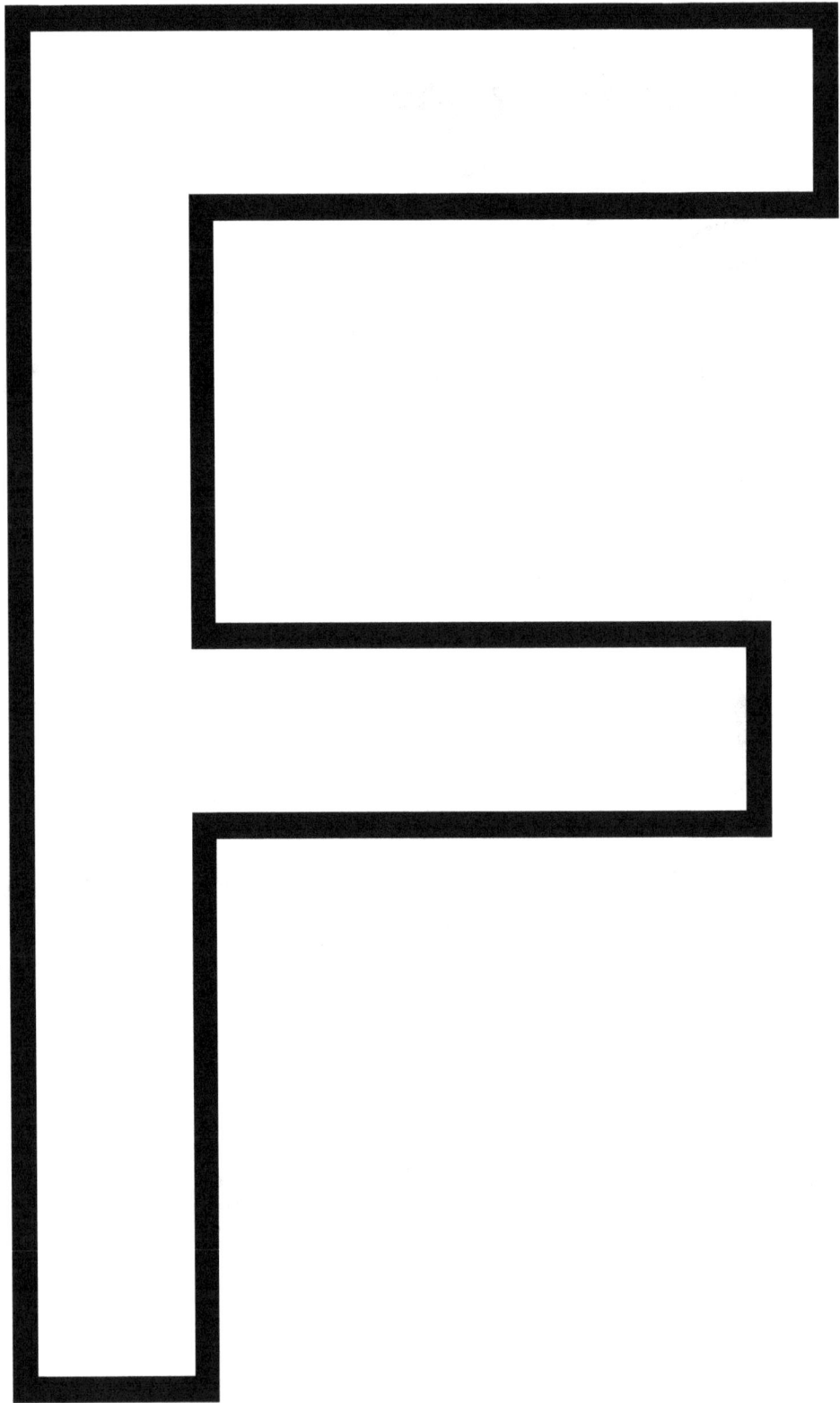

F

Fish

Goat

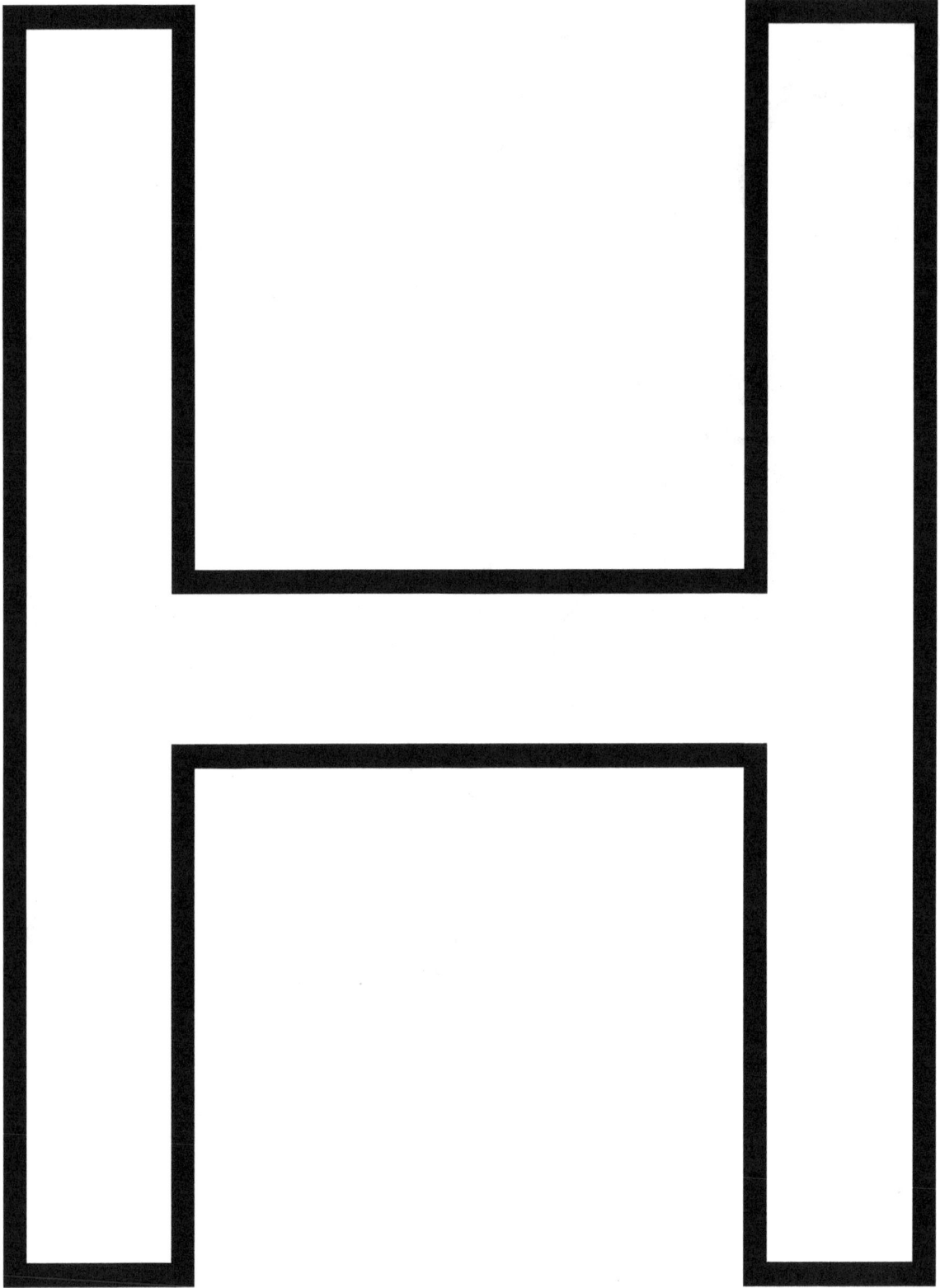

Hummingbird

I

Iguana

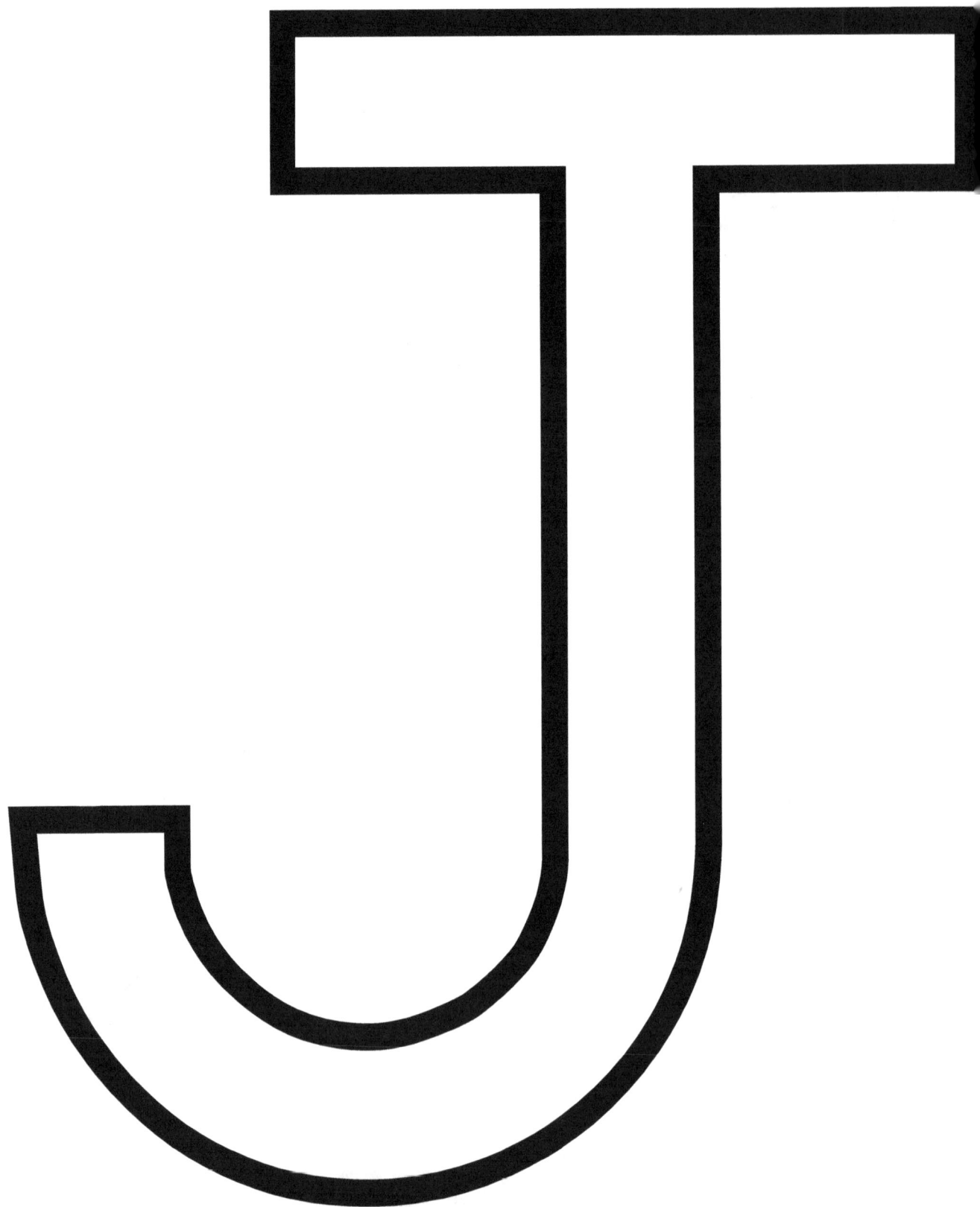

J

Jellyfish

Koala

L

Lobster

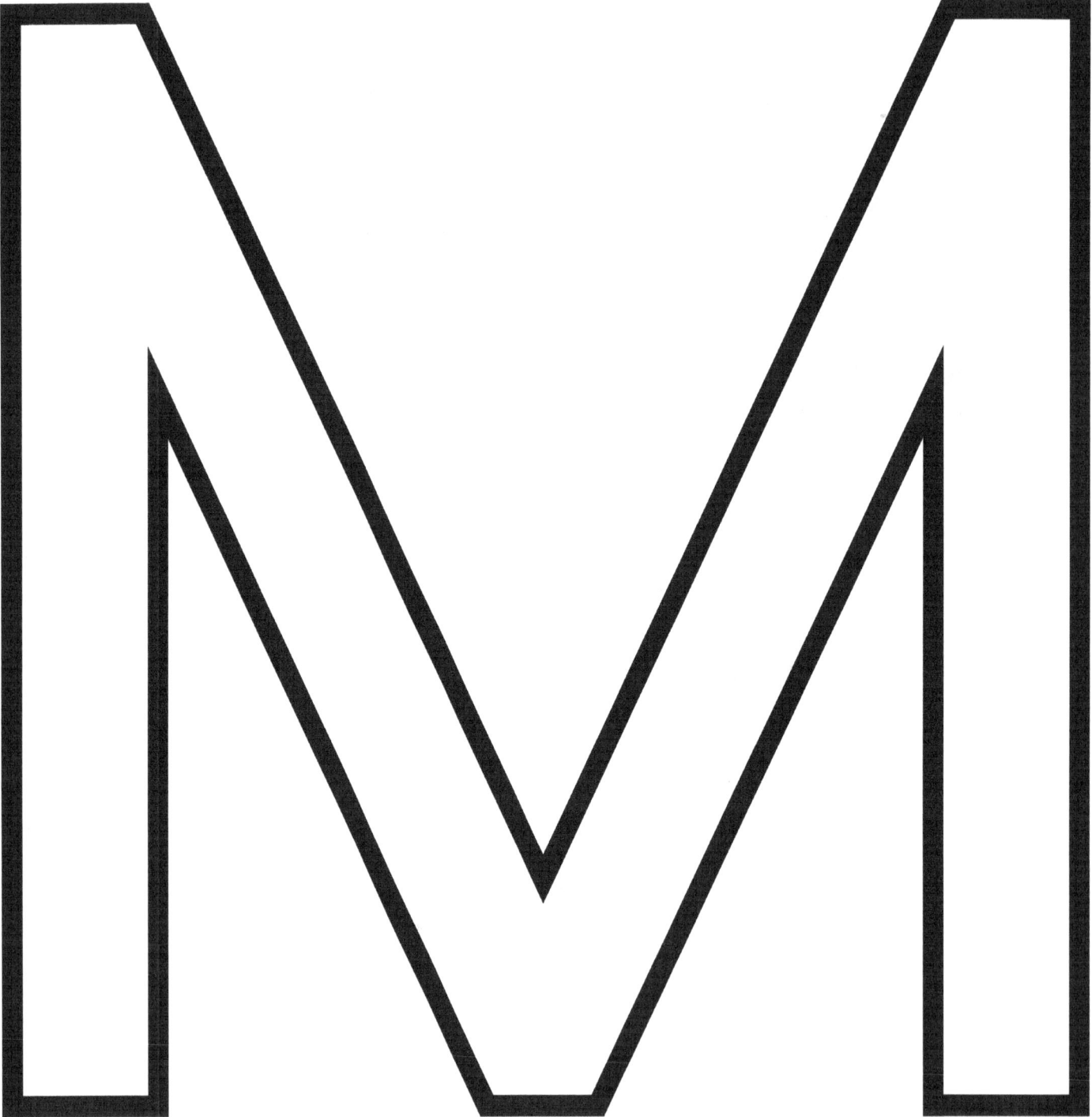

Mouse

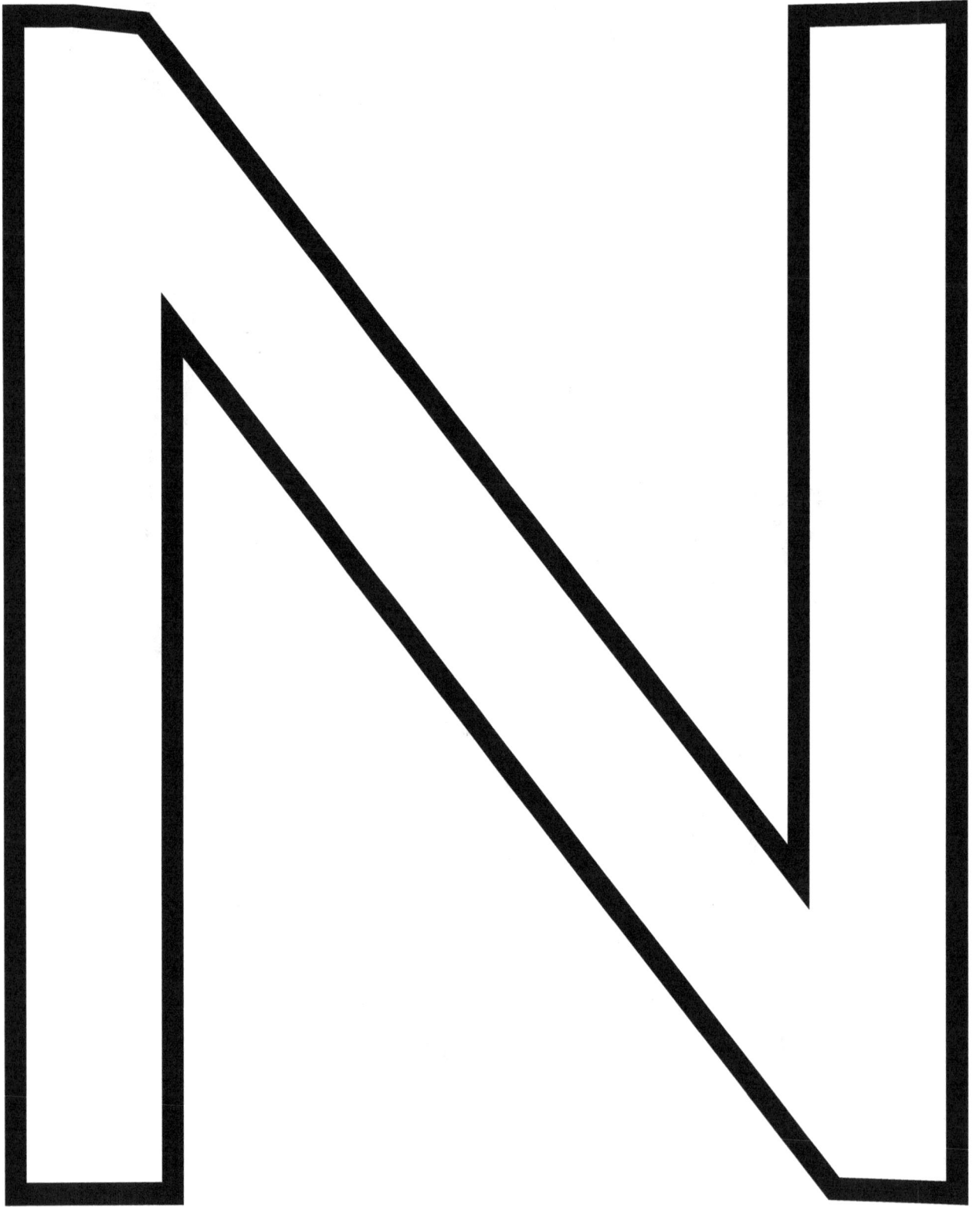

Nightingale

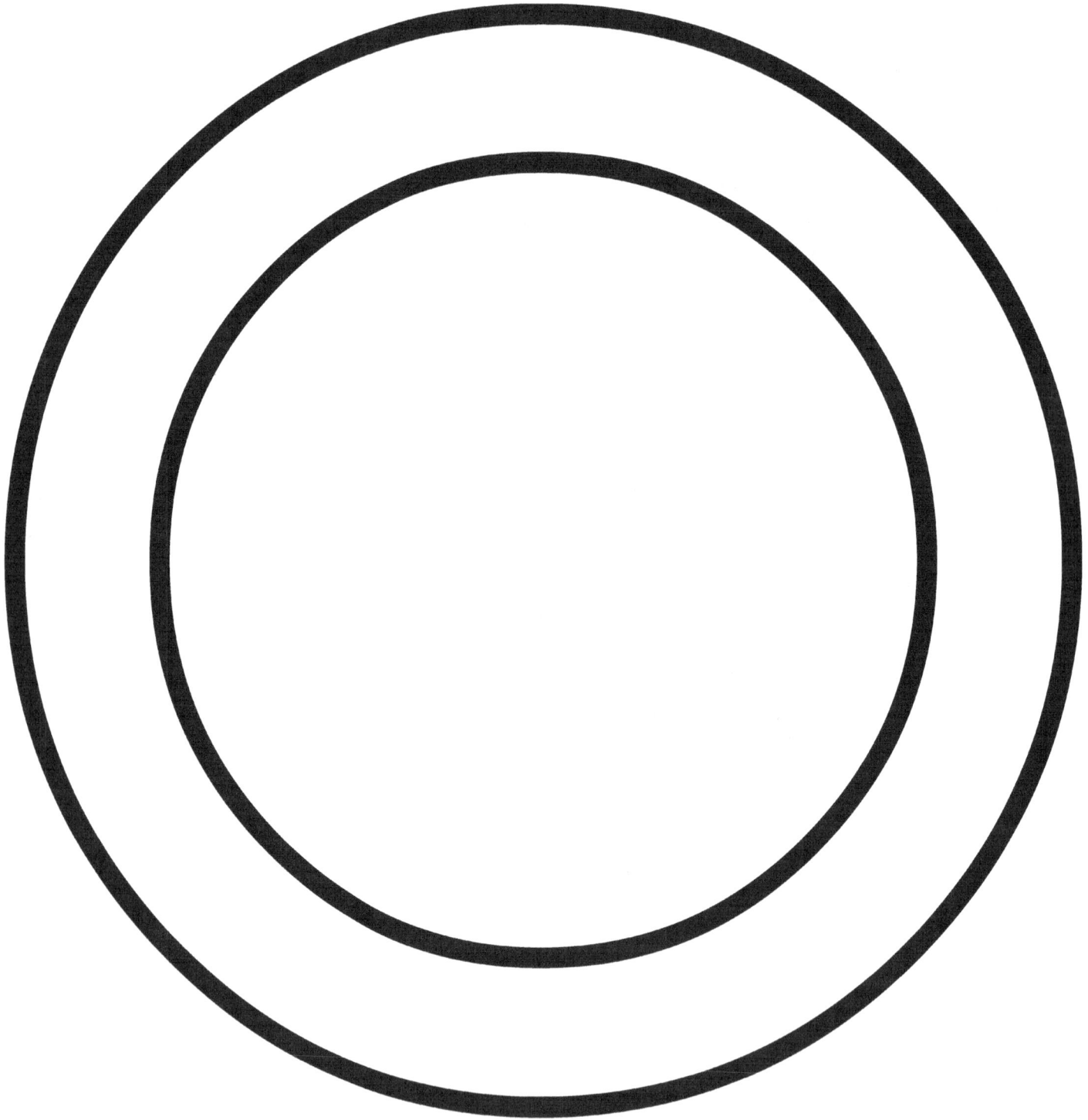

Octopus

P

Porcupine

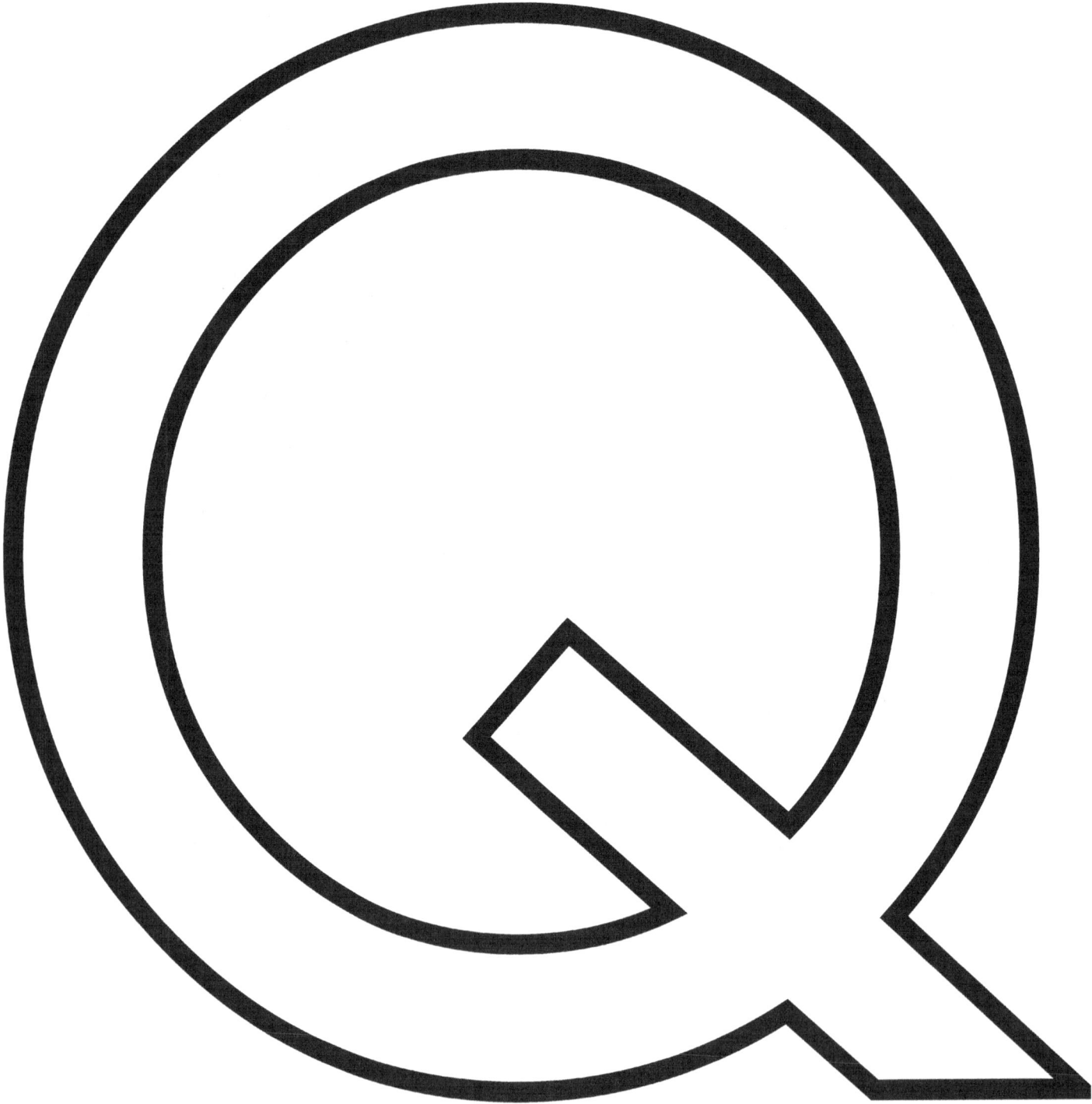

Q

Quail

R

Rooster

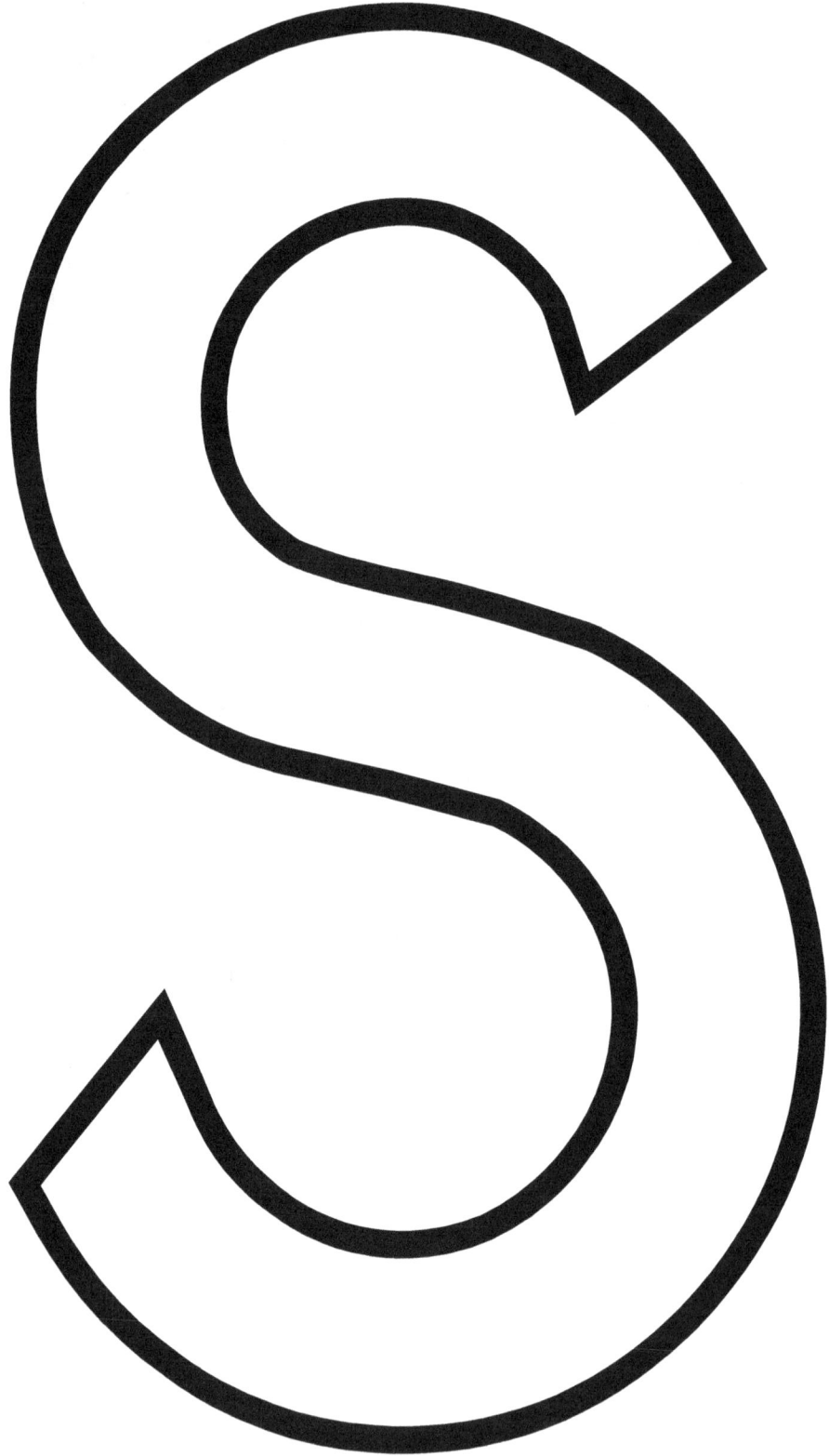

Squirrel

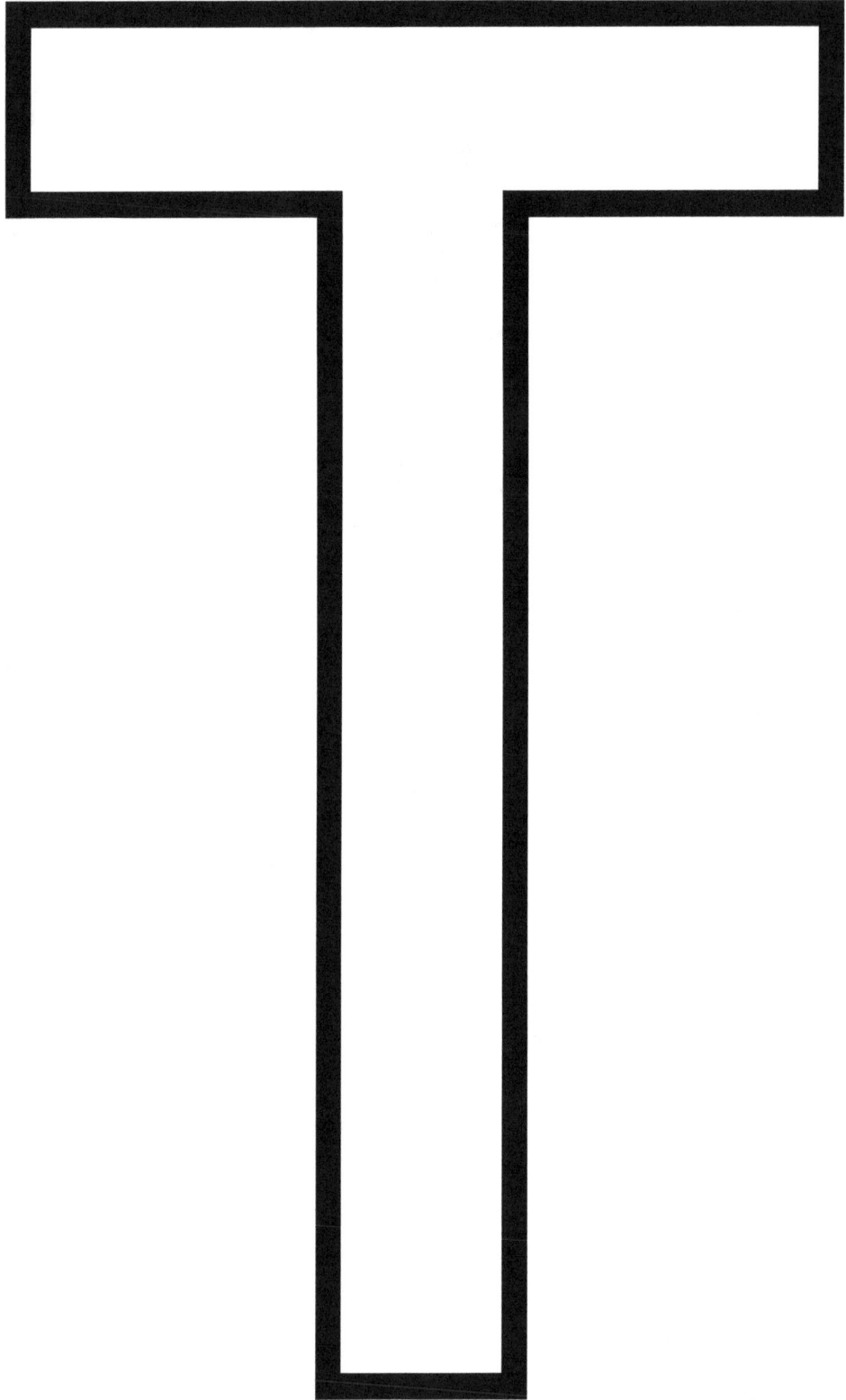

T

Turtle

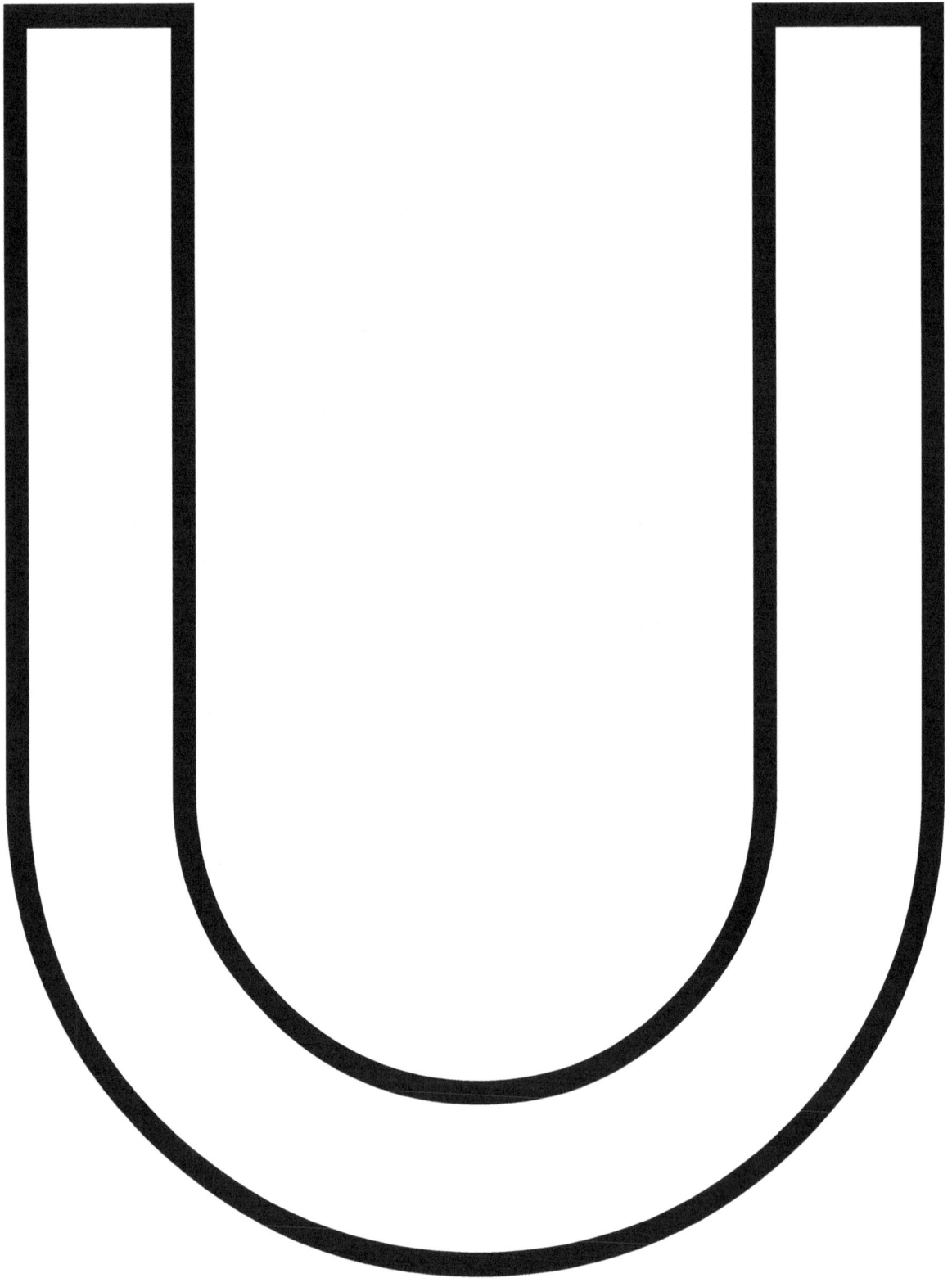

U

Unicorn

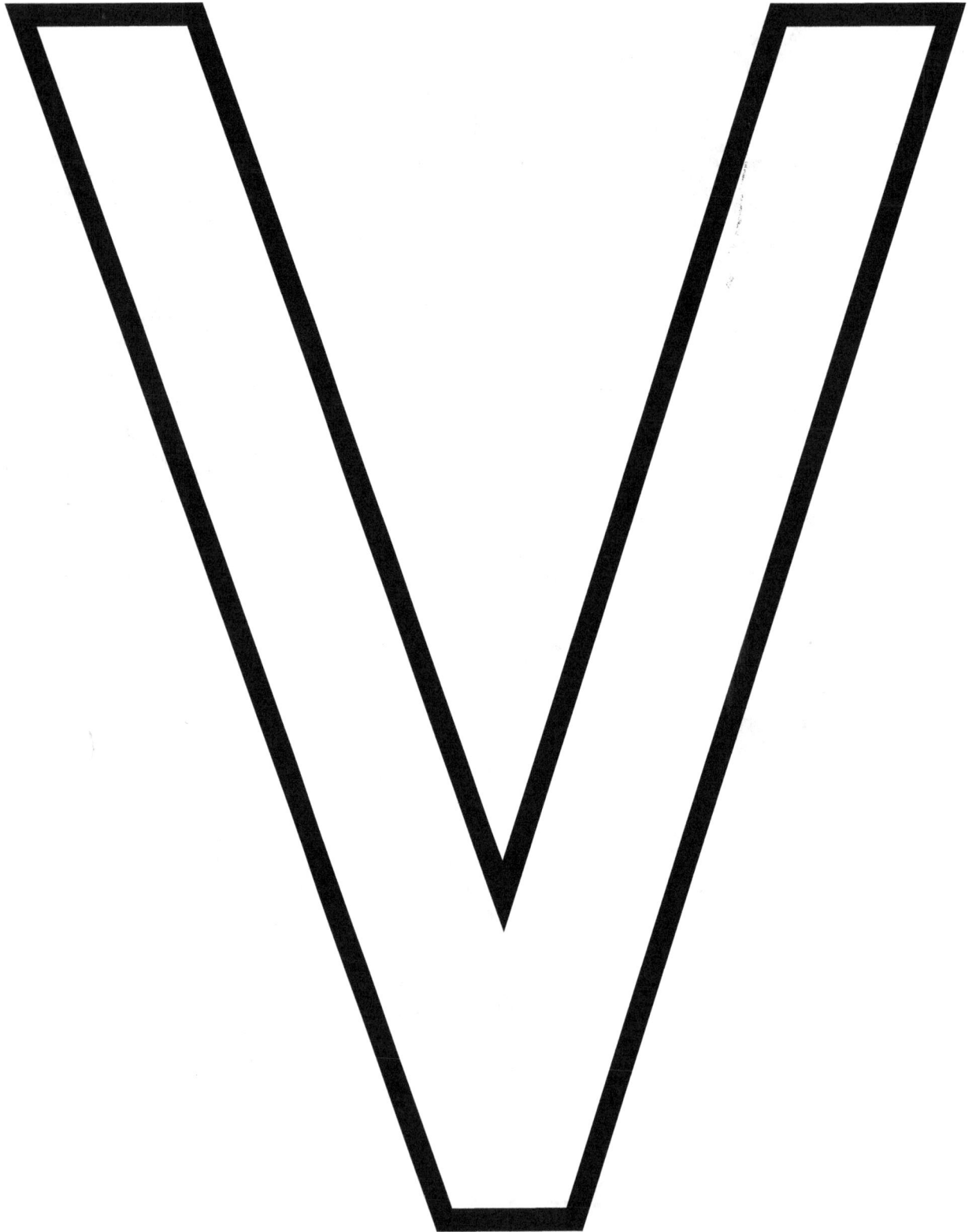

V

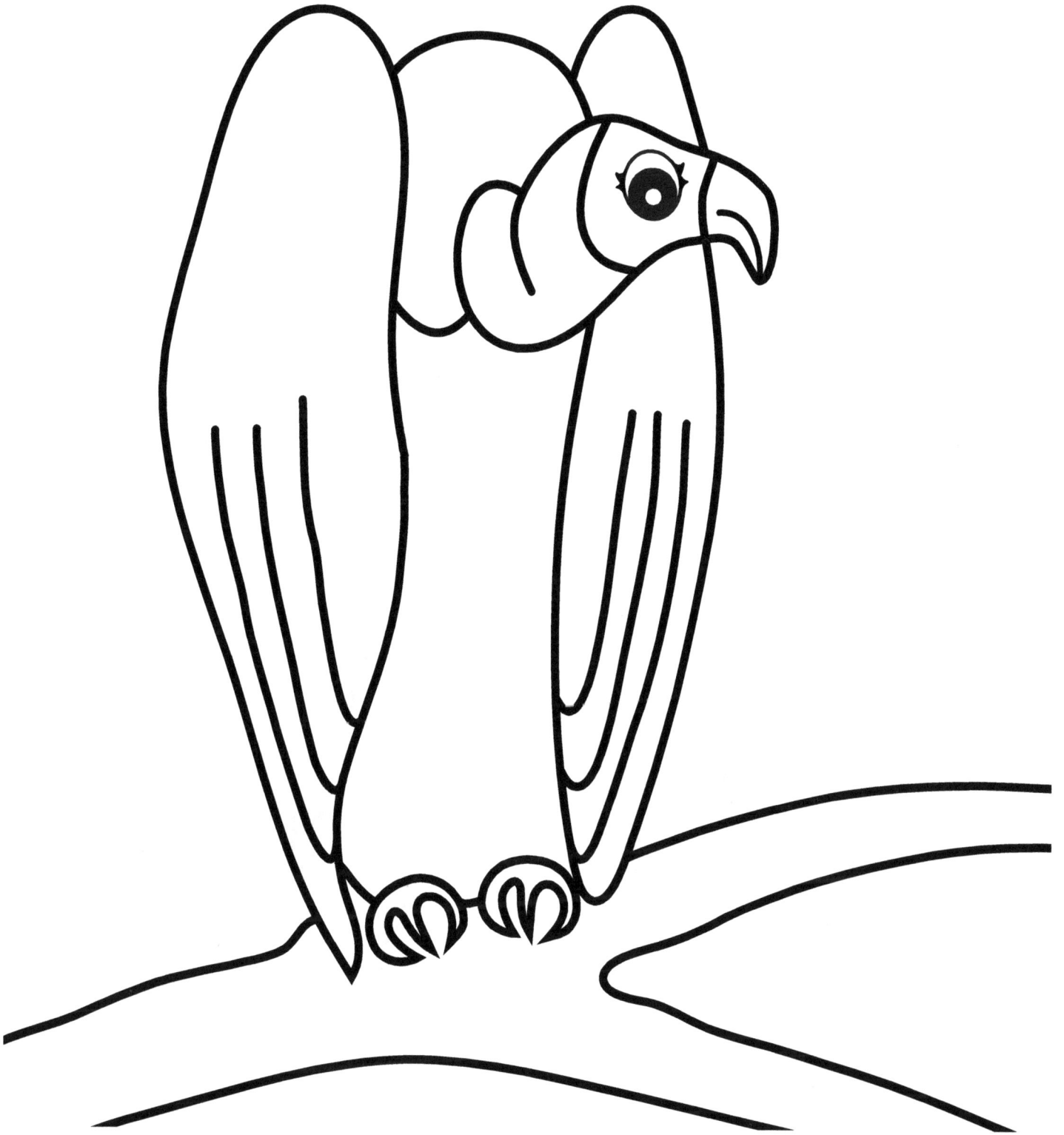

Vulture

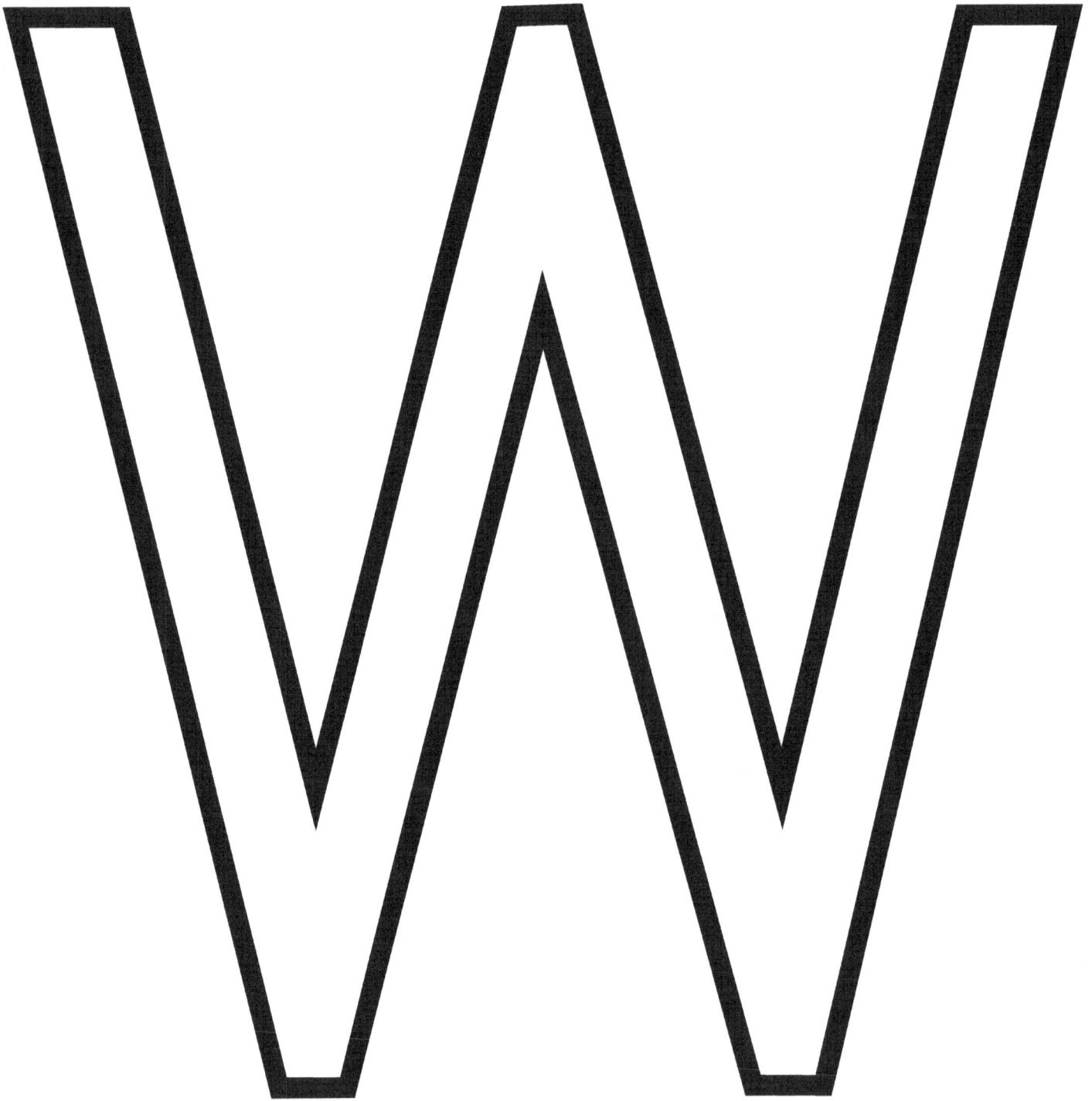

W

Walrus

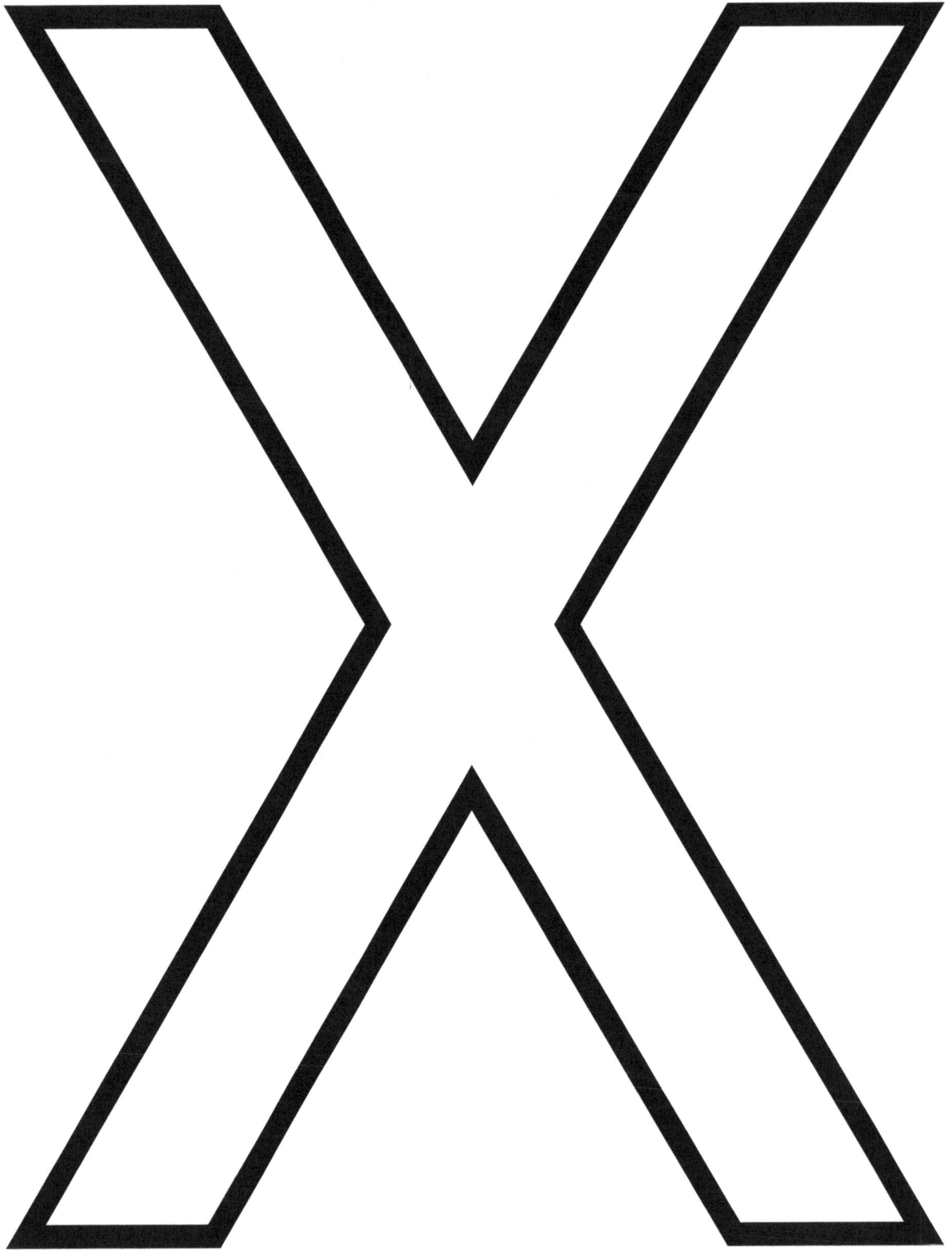

X

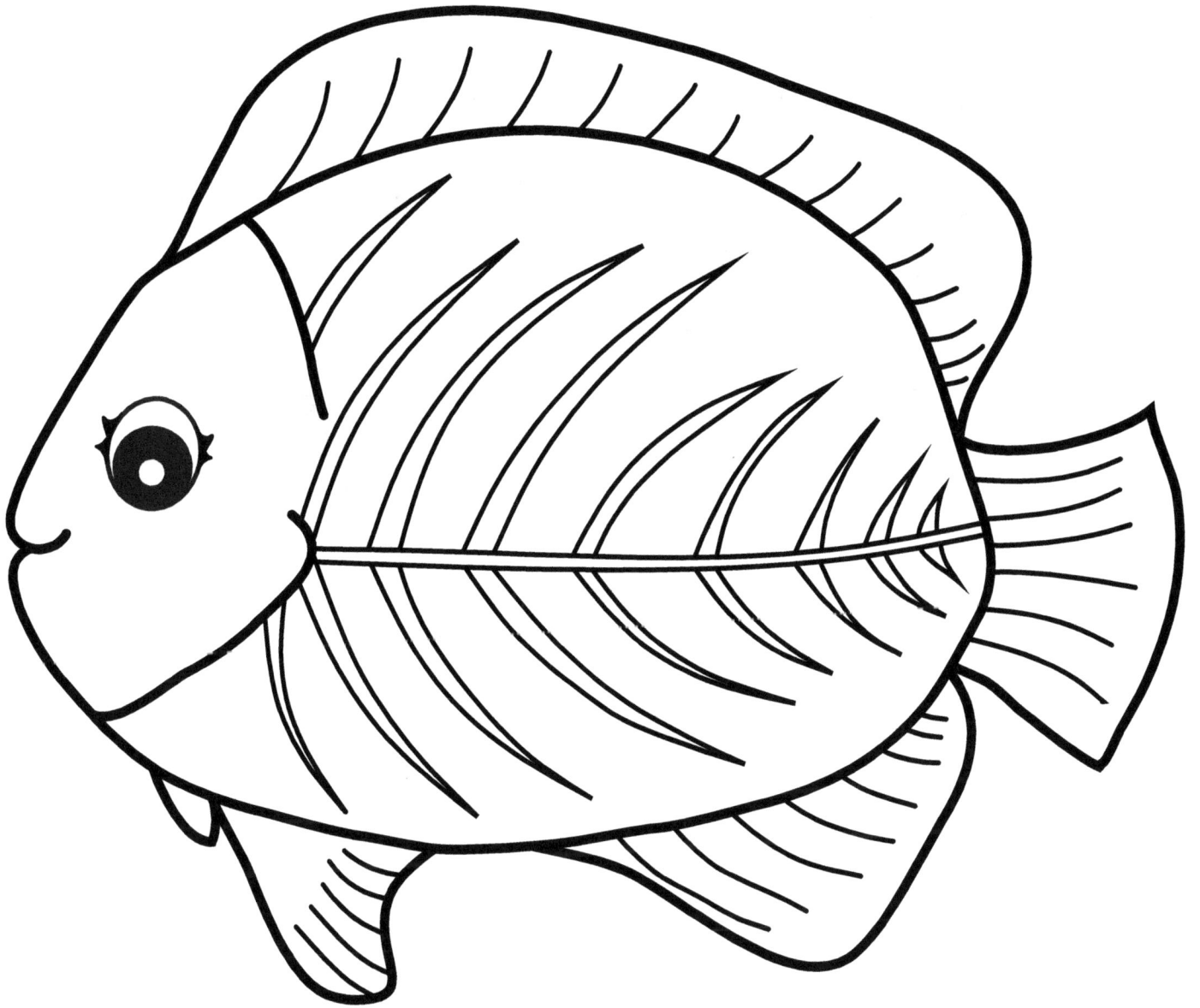

X-Ray Fish

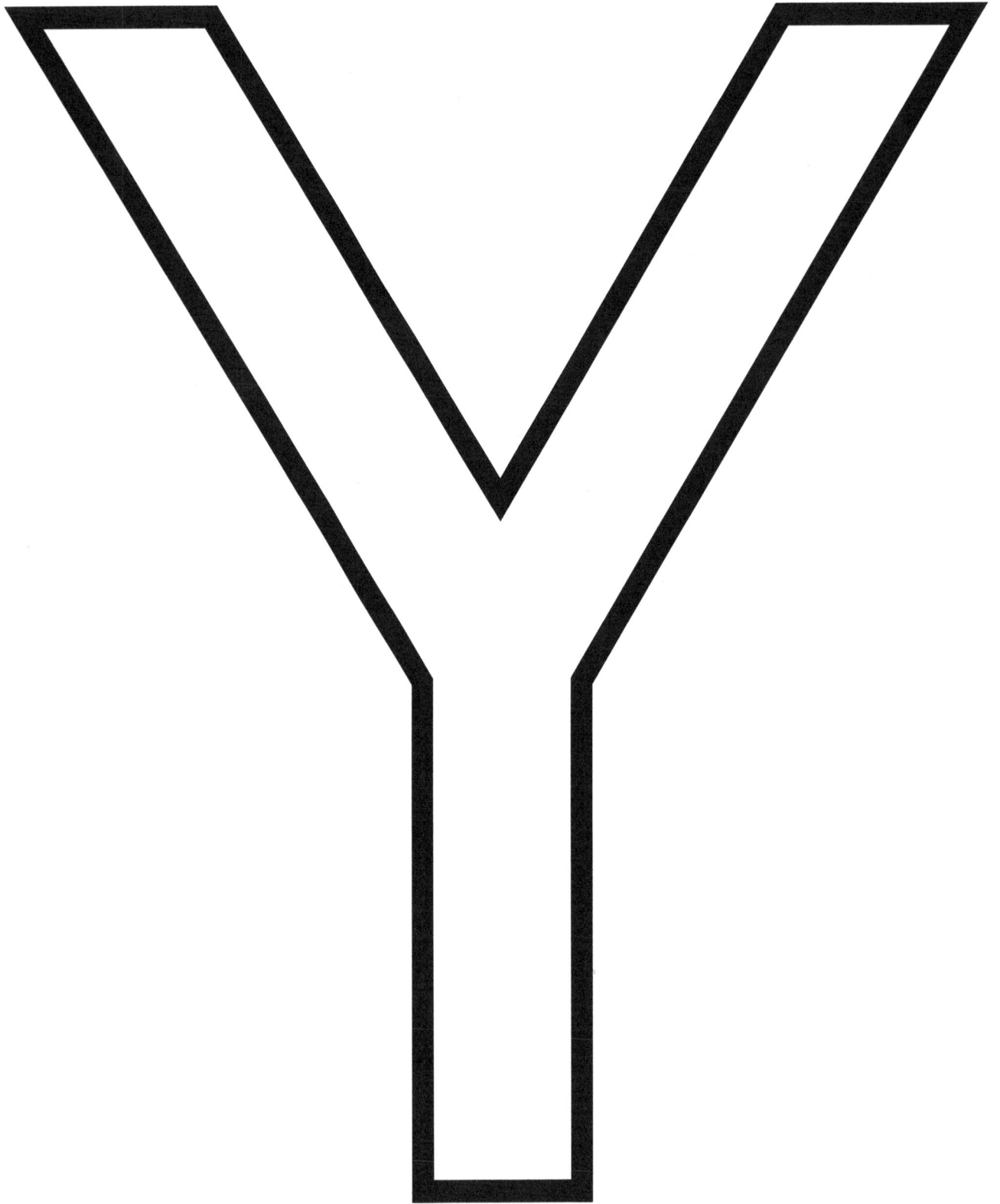

Yak

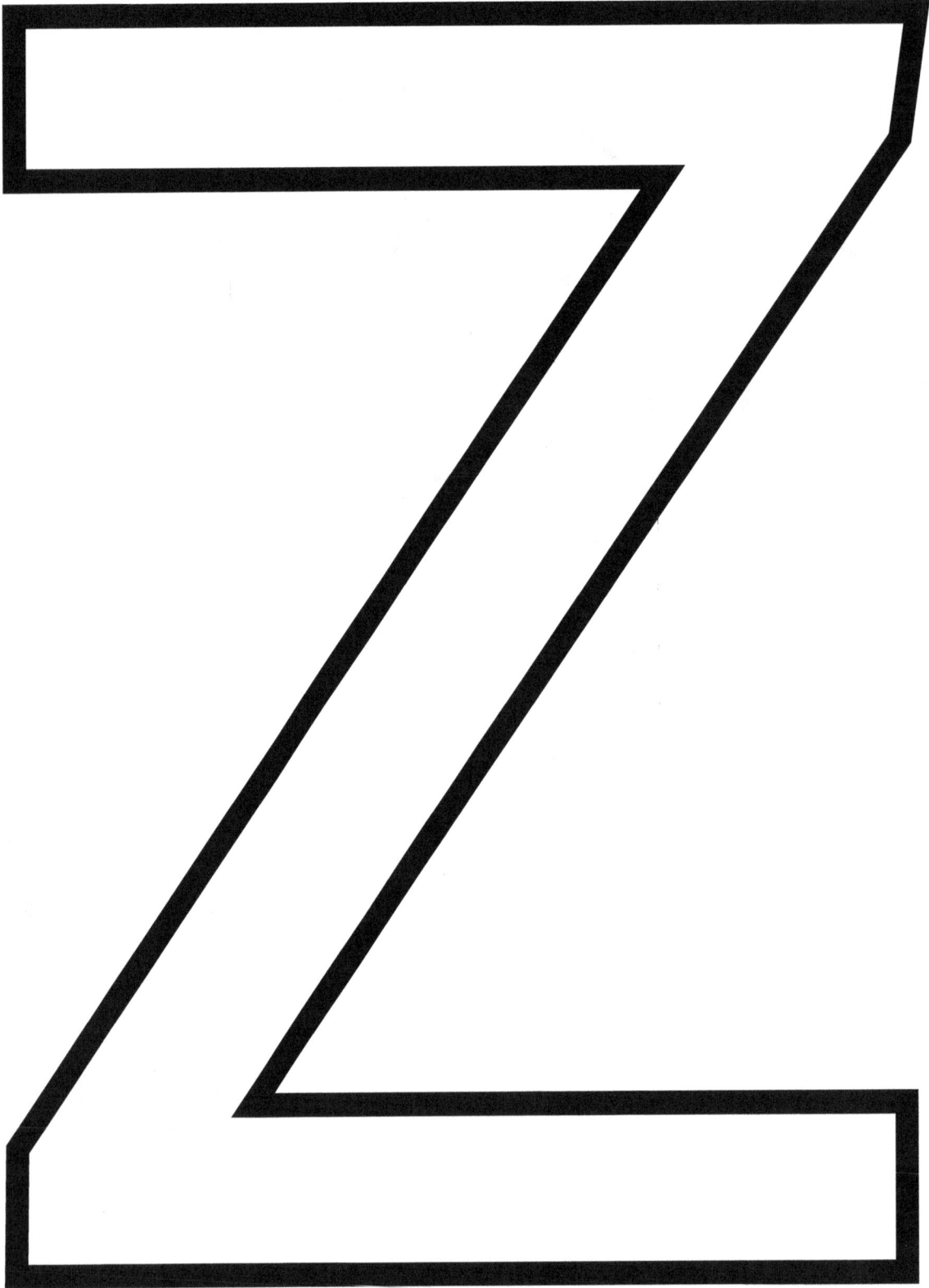

Zebra